Rock Your Wardrobe

Laura Torres

QEB

QEB Publishing

Editor: Eve Marleau
Designer: Lisa Peacock
Photographer: Simon Pask
Project Manager: Dani Hall

Copyright © QEB Publishing, Inc. 2010

Published in the United States by
QEB Publishing, Inc.
3 Wrigley, Suite A
Irvine, CA 92618

www.qed-publishing.co.uk

Library of Congress Cataloging-in-Publication Data

Torres, Laura.
 Wardrobe / Laura Torres.
   p. cm. -- (QEB rock your . .)
 ISBN 978-1-59566-937-7 (library binding)
 1. Dress accessories--Juvenile literature. 2. Children's
clothing--Juvenile literature. I. Title.
 TT649.8.T67 2011
 646.4'06--dc22

                                        2010010671

Printed in China

Contents

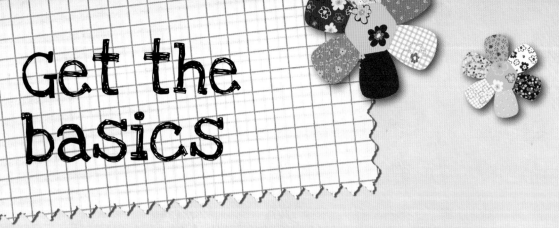

Get the basics

Is your wardrobe full of plain white socks and T-shirts? Help is here! With a few materials and a little crafty instruction, you can turn items in your wardrobe into one-of-a-kind works of art.

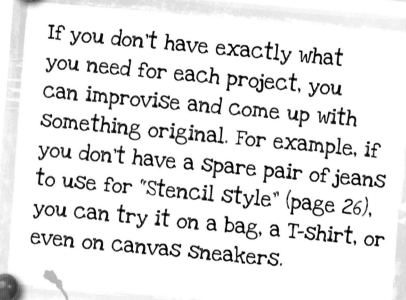

If you don't have exactly what you need for each project, you can improvise and come up with something original. For example, if you don't have a spare pair of jeans to use for "Stencil style" (page 26), you can try it on a bag, a T-shirt, or even on canvas sneakers.

WARNING On pages where you see this symbol, ask an adult for help.

Here are a few of the basic craft items
you will need for some of the projects:

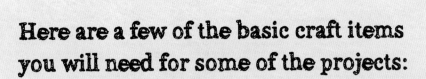

Polymer clay—This is a fun way to make all sorts of beads. You can mix different-colored clays together to make a swirl pattern, then bake according to the packet instructions.

Embroidery floss—Embroidery floss comes in every color you can imagine. Traditional embroidery floss is made up of six or more threads per strand. It also comes as a single, thick strand. Either kind is fine for the projects in this book.

Scissors—Make sure you always have a good pair of scissors for cutting materials such as paper, felt, and yarn in the projects.

Glue—If a project needs "glue" you can use whatever you might have around the house. "White glue" means a white standard glue. "Craft glue" means a thick white glue that won't run or spread.

Always remember...
When making a project, protect the surface you are working on with newspaper or plastic for a mess-free, easy clean-up.

Tie-dye Socks

- White socks
- Fabric dye
- Water
- Plastic bowl
- Rubber bands
- Latex gloves
- Plastic spoon
- Plastic bags

WARNING

Plain white socks get a whole new look with this one-color tie-dye treatment. Add a splash of fun to your feet!

Why not try using a bright-pink dye for stand-out socks?

Step 1

Cover the work area with plastic bags. Prepare the fabric dye in the bowl according to the package instructions.

6

Step 2

Run water over the socks and squeeze it out. Wrap rubber bands around several small sections of the socks.

Step 3

Put the socks in the dye, using the plastic spoon to make sure they are completely covered by the dyed water.

Step 4

Let the socks sit in the dye for about half an hour, stirring them around every now and again with the plastic spoon.

Step 5

Wearing the gloves, remove the socks from the dye and rinse them until the water runs clear. Remove the bands and let the socks dry on plastic bags.

Friendship bracelet

This traditional knotted friendship bracelet has been given a simple twist. You can make lots of them really quickly!

Why not make a bracelet in the colors of your favorite sports team?

Step 1

Cut three strands of each color of embroidery floss to 24 inches (60 centimeters) each. You will have six strands.

Step 2

Tie them all together in a knot, about 1.5 inches (4 centimeters) from one end.

Step 3

Clip the bracelet at the knot end on a clipboard.

Step 4

Pull out one strand. Make a single knot around the rest of the floss. Repeat ten times. Repeat several times with each strand.

Step 5

Repeat with each strand until the bracelet fits around your wrist. Tie a knot at each end then tie the two ends together.

Rubber band belt

YOU WILL NEED

- About 20 large colorful rubber bands, or 40 small colorful rubber bands
- Beads with large holes
- Large button with shank, or stem
- Thread

Weave a fun belt out of colorful rubber bands. You could make a color-coordinated belt to match every pair of trousers!

Try adding gold beads to your belt for a sparkly, party look.

Step 1

Loop one rubber band through another to attach them, then pull tight to secure.

Step 2

Thread a bead onto the second rubber band. Continue looping and beading until the belt fits around your waist.

Step 3

Using a small piece of thread, attach the button to the rubber band.

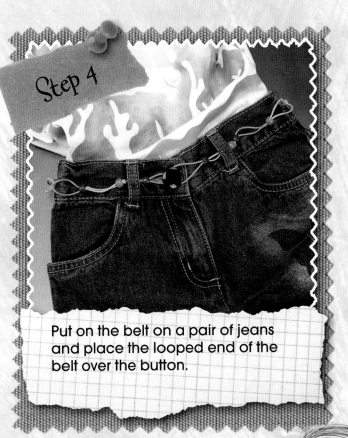

Step 4

Put on the belt on a pair of jeans and place the looped end of the belt over the button.

Chunky bead bracelet

It's easy to make and bake your own clay beads to create stylish bracelets. You can find polymer clay at all good craft stores.

Step 1

Make a thin sausage shape of each of two colors of the clay. Twist the two shapes together.

← Make your bracelet from blues, greens, and grays for a cool camouflage look.

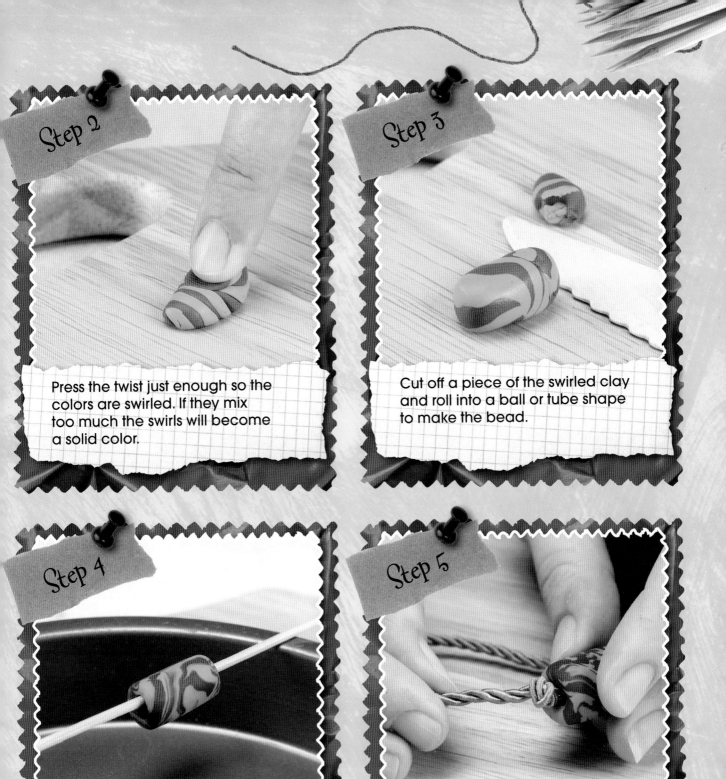

Step 2

Press the twist just enough so the colors are swirled. If they mix too much the swirls will become a solid color.

Step 3

Cut off a piece of the swirled clay and roll into a ball or tube shape to make the bead.

Step 4

Poke a hole in the bead with the toothpick and set across the top of the dish on the skewer. Bake according to the package instructions.

Step 5

When the bead is cool, thread it onto the cord and tie a knot on either side of the bead. Tie the ends to make a bracelet.

Rainbow shoelaces

Spice up your sneakers with these colorful laces. All you need is some brightly colored embroidery floss.

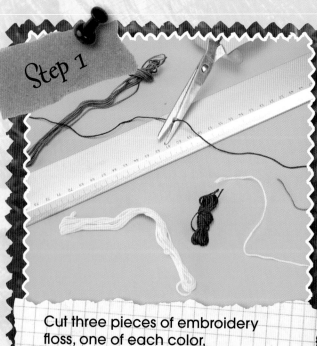

Step 1

Cut three pieces of embroidery floss, one of each color, about 3.3 feet (1 meter) long.

Step 2

Gather the floss together and tie a knot at one end, leaving a tail about 1.2 inches (3 centimeters) long.

Step 3

Tack the end of the thread to a sturdy surface. Keeping all three strands tight, braid the floss.

Step 4

Tie a knot at the end, leaving a tail of at least 1.2 inches (3 centimeters). Unpin the opposite end.

Step 5

Cut a piece of duct tape then wrap it around the floss at each end. Make another lace and tie up your sneakers!

Look for pink and yellow floss to give your sneakers a summery feel!

stringy scarf

Don't throw away your old T-shirts. You can **easily** make them into fun, fashionable scarves instead!

Tie several knots in your scarf to give it a rocky edge!

Step 1

Lay the T-shirt out on a flat surface. Cut off the hem section. Cut the T-shirt into horizontal strips, about 2.5 inches (5 centimeters) wide.

Step 2

Cut each loop open. If your T-shirt has side seams, cut on each side of the seam and throw the seam part away.

Step 3

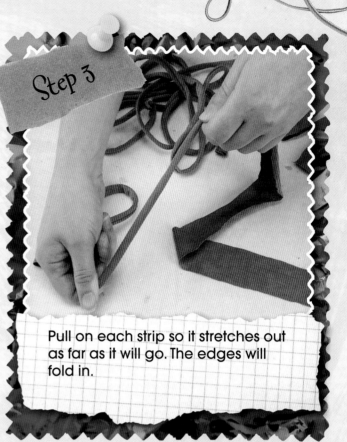

Pull on each strip so it stretches out as far as it will go. The edges will fold in.

Step 4

Gather all the strips together and tie them in a knot in the middle.

Step 5

Plait the strips or leave them loose. Wear the scarf with the knot at the back of your neck.

Designed by you T-shirt

YOU WILL NEED
- Plain white T-shirt
- Thick white craft glue
- Cardboard
- Fabric paint
- Sponge
- Pen
- Paper
- Scissors

Using glue and fabric paint, you can create a cool, one-of-a-kind design for a T-shirt.

➡ Make a flowery T-shirt design for a fun-in-the-sun look.

Step 1

Practice your design on some paper. Cut cardboard to fit inside the T-shirt—this stops the glue and paint touching the back.

Step 2

Draw your design on the T-shirt with the glue. Let it dry completely.

Step 3

Squirt some fabric paint onto a piece of aluminum foil. Dip the sponge into the paint and blot on the foil.

Step 4

Sponge the paint all around the design, making sure to cover the area around the glue completely. Let dry overnight.

Step 5

Soak the T-shirt in water for about 5 minutes, until the glue becomes soft and you can peel it off easily.

Cool cotton bag

With basic sewing skills, you can turn an old T-shirt into a bag for lightweight items. Make sure you ask an adult to help you as needles can be very sharp.

Step 1

→ Jazz up your T-shirt bag by painting a pattern on the front with fabric paint.

Cut a rectangle from the front of the T-shirt, and another one from the back of the T-shirt.

Step 2

Place the rectangles with the design facing inward and pin the pieces together. Sew along one side of the rectangles.

Step 3

Open up the rectangles and fold down the top edges about 2.5 inches (5 centimeters). Pin and sew the folded part close to the edge.

Step 4

Pin the rectangles back together. Sew seams along the bottom and the other side.

Step 5

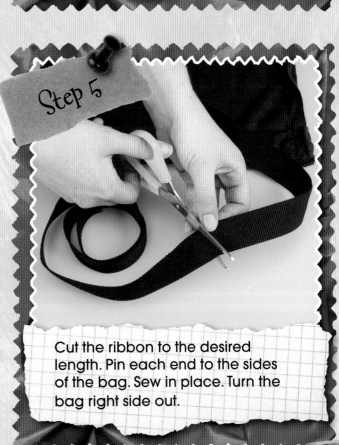

Cut the ribbon to the desired length. Pin each end to the sides of the bag. Sew in place. Turn the bag right side out.

Tile pendant

If you have some old board game pieces around the house, you can make a cool tile pendant necklace.

YOU WILL NEED

- Board game tile or small domino
- Paper or fabric image
- Scissors
- Paintbrush
- Thin ribbon or cord
- Glue
- Beads
- Pen

Step 1

Cut the paper image a bit smaller than the tile. To do this, trace the tile on the paper and then cut just inside the lines.

Step 2

Paint a thin coat of glue on the top of the tile. Stick the image onto the tile, then paint another coat over it. Let dry.

Make a rock star necklace by using a skull and crossbones image and black cord.

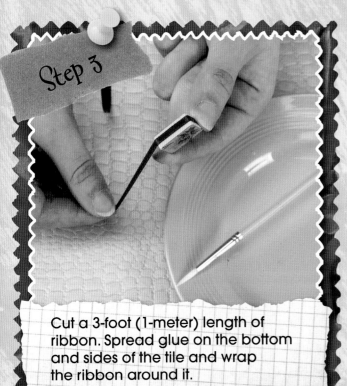

Step 3

Cut a 3-foot (1-meter) length of ribbon. Spread glue on the bottom and sides of the tile and wrap the ribbon around it.

Step 4

Tie a knot in the ribbon at the top of the tile and thread on some beads. Tie the ends of the ribbon to make a necklace.

23

Snazzy Sneakers

Use some metallic permanent markers to personalize your sneakers. You're sure to stand out from the crowd!

Try using several different-colored markers on your sneakers.

Step 1

Clean your sneakers with a damp cloth, making sure you remove all mud or marks.

Step 2

Practice drawing a design on paper first. Large shapes and designs work best. Try bubble letters or shapes and swirls.

Step 3

Draw the design on to the sneakers with a pencil. Trace over your design with metallic permanent markers.

Step 4

You can also draw around the edge of the sole. When you have finished, try them on!

stencil style

Make a fashion statement with a reverse stencil technique that looks good on T-shirts or jeans.

Step 1

Draw some designs on the self-adhesive paper, then cut them out.

Step 2

Peel off the back of the paper and stick the stencils securely onto the jeans.

↑

Create an underwater world with blues and greens.

Step 4

Squeeze some fabric paint onto a paper plate. Dip a sponge in the paint and dab around the design. Let dry.

Step 5

Carefully remove the paper to reveal your design, then try on your new-look jeans!

Pretty-as-a-picture pendant

Who knew an ordinary door hinge could look so good? All you need is some colorful gift wrap and ribbon.

YOU WILL NEED

- Small hinge (can be bought at all DIY shops)
- Cord or ribbon
- Card
- Gift wrap
- Scissors
- Glue
- Small picture

Step 1

Cut a piece of ribbon long enough to go around your neck. Thread it through the upper left hole of the hinge.

Step 2

Tie a knot in the ribbon, just above the hole, to secure it.

Step 3

Cut some card and gift wrap slightly smaller than the hinge. Glue the paper on the card, then glue it onto the hinge.

Step 4

Cut the picture on another piece of card to fit inside the hinge, then glue the card to the hinge.

Step 5

Once the glue has dried, tie the ends of the ribbon together to make a necklace.

Why not make your pendant into a backpack accessory by threading it through a keyring?

Many of the projects in this book are perfect for party activities. Here are a few ideas.

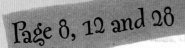

Pages 6 and 18

Overnight stays

For sleepover parties, you can make tie-dye socks or designed-by-you T-shirts. Buy inexpensive packs of white socks and T-shirts and provide several colors of dye for the socks, and several colors of fabric paint for the T-shirts. You can make the socks or T-shirts the night before and let them dry overnight before guests take them home, or wear them the next day.

Page 8, 12 and 28

Party favors

Chunky bead bracelets and tile pendants are great for a large party because the supplies are inexpensive and they are easy for everyone to make.

Firm friends

To make funky friendship bracelets, give each person a safety pin to secure the knot to the leg of their trousers, instead of using a clipboard. Supply several colors of thread to choose from. At the end of the party, guests can swap bracelets.

Party accessories

Ask everyone to bring an old T-shirt to your party so you can make T-shirt scarves. Cut up the T-shirts and swap strips so everyone has a matching, colorful scarf.

The perfect present

Make a pair of snazzy sneakers as a gift for the birthday boy or girl. Everyone can sign their name on the sneakers for a lasting keepsake.

Index